MW01519207

You Can't Keep Jesus In The Nativity Scene

Sunday School Christmas Program

Cynthia E. Cowen

CSS Publishing Company, Inc., Lima, Ohio

YOU CAN'T KEEP JESUS IN THE NATIVITY SCENE

For more information about CSS Publishing Company resources, visit our website at
www.csspub.com.

ISBN 0-7880-1839-6   PRINTED IN U.S.A.

Even a child is known by his actions, by whether his conduct is pure and right.   Proverbs 20:11 (NIV)

I dedicate this resource to my son, Justin Edwin Paul Cowen, who is my Mr. Lost N. Foundit. His actions reflect a pure and right conduct. Even though he is a preacher's kid, Justin found a faith for himself in Jesus Christ, our Lord, at a very early age. His faithfulness in worship and to enhancing the Kingdom of God is an example to others and an encouragement to his parents.

Justin is there to rescue me when I can't find the tool bar or have deleted a program from the computer. He is there when I need an older youth to do special speaking in a program. He is willing to accompany younger youth to retreats. He is a fine example to others of a committed Christian. I thank him for his sacrifice of time when I have been involved in my writing. I thank him for the times of fun playing games, watching a movie, or just hanging out with his mom. I am very grateful for all the hugs and love which we continue to exchange even as he grows into adulthood.

Justin, know you are very loved and honored for being a loving son!

Your Mom

Table Of Contents

Foreword

This program is designed for use as a Christmas pageant for a large or small congregation. Two of the main characters, Ms. Arranger and Mr. Lost N. Foundit, dialogue with each other as the youth sing the message of the Christmas story and that Jesus loves each one of us.

You Can't Keep Jesus In The Nativity Scene is a message which is relevant to our society and church in the present age. The Lord cannot be contained in a manger scene. Jesus is alive and well and moving in our world today. You can find him wherever there is a need and love to be shared.

Script

You Can't Keep Jesus In The Nativity Scene

Script For Ms. Arranger And Mr. Lost N. Foundit

Christmas Prelude

Welcome And Announcements

Sunday School Superintendent

Opening Prayer   Pastor

Special Music

Opening Reader   Matthew 4:16-17
"Although your people live in darkness, they will see a bright light. Although they live in the shadow of death, a light will shine on them ... turn back to God! The kingdom of heaven will soon be here."

(Reader exits. Mary and Joseph take their places at the manger.)

Ms. Arranger: *(Enters from the side wearing a hat decorated in Christmas fashion and red or green vest with button that says, Holiday Tours.)* Lights! Action! Good afternoon, everyone. I've come out from the dark to share a great afternoon celebration with you! I'm Ms. Arranger from Holiday Tours. I've been commissioned to guide your congregation through your Children's Christmas Pageant. This is a new thing for me. I don't really go to church anywhere. Most places I've tried don't do things the way *I want* to see them done. And their activities and worship? Well, they don't quite fit in to my busy life. So this time with you should be interesting.

The first stop I've been asked to make here is at your nativity scene. I've been told that your custodian has it all set up. I'll just take my trusty flashlight (*Pulls out light and shines it.*) and look around this area until I locate all the pieces. While I'm looking around, let's hear from you, congregation, about the birthplace of this baby called the Christ Child.

Congregation   "O Little Town Of Bethlehem"
(*Pre-school, Kindergarten, and First Grade come in.*)

Ms. Arranger: (*Steps to the nativity scene.*) Well, here is the nativity scene, just as I was told. And there seems to be a large group of children wanting to tell me about it. Let's listen to what they have to tell us of this manger scene.

Pre-school, Kindergarten, and First Grade
                                         "Away In A Manger"

Ms. Arranger: A child in a manger. Interesting ... why on earth would a mother put her brand new baby in a feeding trough for animals? And by the way, where is that baby? I only count a Mary and a Joseph in your scene. Isn't there suppose to be this baby called Jesus in all nativity scenes? Jesus, oh, Jesus, where are you? (*Shines her light out looking for Christ.*)

Youth   "Jesus Loves Me" (v. 1)

Ms. Arranger: I didn't *arrange* for that song, you cute little darlings, but thank you for the reminder that Jesus loves each one of us. But, you'll have a hard time convincing folk that he exists if we don't find him and put him back in that manger. It looks so empty. So on your way out, look down the aisles for that baby Jesus. Would you?

Congregation   "God Rest Ye Merry Gentlemen"
(*Children exit.*)

Ms. Arranger: "Gone astray" ... is that what those children were singing about? Oh, Jesus, I wish I could find you. (*Sighs heavily*

10

and shines the light on the empty manger. Sighs again and sings "Jesus loves me" — *pauses* — "this I know" — *pauses*.)

I remember hearing about Jesus when I was the age of those children. When did I lose him? Just got too busy and misplaced him in my life, I guess. I know I've been away from church and God too long, but right now I have to find his infant form. (*Shines light around looking for Jesus*.)

Excuse me for a minute. I'm going off to find (*names church's custodian*) — your church custodian. While I'm gone, why don't you listen to the second graders sing a Christmas song?

Come on in, young people, and do your thing. I just have to go arrange for (*name of custodian in your church*) to locate that babe that's supposed to be in this Christmas scene. (*Steps to the side to look for custodian*.)

Congregation   "What Child Is This?" (vv. 1-2)
(*Second graders come in with Mr. Lost N. Foundit, dressed in trench coat, hat, and carrying baby Jesus, who places doll in manger and steps to side while youth sing. Ms. Arranger appears again*.)

Second Graders   "Hark! The Herald Angels Sing" (vv. 1 and 3)

Ms. Arranger: Hmmmm ... God and sinners reconciled — brought back together. That's a thought-provoking message. I know God didn't leave me. I've just been so busy arranging things for myself that I sort of left God out of the picture. And I can see right now, life would have been better if he had been there. Well, would you look at that! The baby Jesus came back to the nativity scene. How'd he get there?

Mr. Lost N. Foundit: (*Steps out of the shadows*.) I brought him back. Got a report that he was missing.

Ms. Arranger: And who are you? I didn't arrange for a private eye to find Jesus. Before you tell me your tale though, I need to dismiss these young people. (*A student from the group steps up and hands her a slip of paper*.) But what's this note? It appears these shy doves want to sing for me again. Okay, it's not on my list of arrangements, but I suppose you could. Let's hear it.

Second Graders   "Jesus Loves Me" (v. 1)

Ms. Arranger: If I were the suspicious kind, I'd think someone was sending me a message about becoming a child again so I could understand that Jesus loves me. Okay ... okay ... I'm listening, God. You children can return to your seats now. We've found Jesus — that is, we've found the baby Jesus for the manger scene. Congregation, sing them home.

Congregation   "It Came Upon The Midnight Clear" (vv. 1, 4)
(*Children exit.*)

Ms. Arranger: Peace ... that's what's been missing in my life for so long. I want to hire you as my own private eye to look for my *missing peace.*

Mr. Lost N. Foundit: You may have a *piece* of you missing, but only God can fill that hole you have in your heart with his peace. But let me introduce myself. (*Hands her his calling card.*) I just happen to be a Public Eye, not a Private Eye. The name is Mr. Lost N. Foundit, and I've had my eye on this Jesus a long time. In fact, he's the reason I'm no longer lost.

Ms. Arranger: Oh, so you were lost but now you're found? I think I still don't have all the pieces put together in my life yet to see a clear picture of Jesus so I'm still lost. Can God possibly find me?

Mr. Lost N. Foundit: You bet he can. And when the Spirit opens your eyes, wow! Jesus and his love for you will be crystal clear.

Ms. Arranger: But back to our missing Jesus. Has he ever disappeared before?

Mr. Lost N. Foundit: Now that you mention it, he's been very active. This isn't the first time that Jesus has been missing from the nativity scene. Last week I found him at the hospital.

Ms. Arranger: Was he ill?

Mr. Lost N. Foundit: No, he was visiting one of the members of this church who was.

Ms. Arranger: And who brought him back?

Mr. Lost N. Foundit: Someone who felt nudged to go visit the sick lady that day. He found Jesus in her arms. She was sleeping all cozy like — at complete peace.

Ms. Arranger: It was nice of Jesus to make a house call, but that baby should be in the nativity scene — not in a sick bed.

Mr. Lost N. Foundit: But that's exactly where Jesus would turn up. Healing the sick — giving comfort and hope to those who need him.

Ms. Arranger: Well, I think I need another song to help me focus on this scene before me. I like to keep Jesus in his own little box, you know ... baby Jesus in the manger. The idea of Jesus running around this town is too much. Come on, congregation, bring on some more of those little children to sing to us.

Congregation   "The First Noel" (vv. 1 and 2)
(*Third and Fourth Graders enter.*)

Third and Fourth Graders   "O Come, Little Children"

Ms. Arranger: There's that message again: to come as a child to Jesus. But you children look like you have another message for me. What is it?

Third and Fourth Graders   "Jesus Loves Me" (v. 1)

Ms. Arranger: Reading the Bible ... I probably should do more of it.

Mr. Lost N. Foundit: And what about your prayer time?

Ms. Arranger: Prayer ... I should arrange more time in my life for that, too, but right now I have to *arrange* for these children to exit. Let's hear verses 3 and 4 of that last song you just sang, congregation.

Congregation   "The First Noel" (vv. 3 and 4)
(*Children exit.*)

Mr. Lost N. Foundit: Well, Ms. Arranger, let me tell you that since I found time to read the Bible and pray each day, I've felt a lot closer to God. And in this busy time of the year, prayer is so important to keep one focused on the reason for the season. Which reminds me of another place I found Jesus.

Ms. Arranger: You mean you can't seem to keep Jesus in the nativity scene. So where was it that you found him?

Mr. Lost N. Foundit: Of all places, over at Super One (*name of your local grocery store*) on the canned goods aisle. He was in someone's cart.

Ms. Arranger: Was he a part of her shopping list?

Mr. Lost N. Foundit: As a matter of fact he was. The lady who had the cart was buying canned goods for the local food pantry. Christmas is a great time for Christians to give.

Ms. Arranger: It is. I've even found myself picking up some extra cans of corn to put into hands of those soliciting for shelters. It makes my heart warm, and I feel like singing. But I don't want to do it alone. Let's bring out some more young hearts as the congregation sings our next Christmas carol.

Congregation   "Angels We Have Heard On High" (vv. 1-3)
(*Fifth and Sixth Graders enter.*)

Fifth and Sixth Graders
                        "Good Christian Friends, Rejoice" (vv. 1-3)

Ms. Arranger: "Christ was born to save"... and what's that mean? I'm supposed to become like a baby again and get "reborn" so maybe God will accept a *better* me?

Mr. Lost N. Foundit: Yes, according to the Bible, we all need to have a "new birth"... to turn from arranging things in our lives and let God do the programming. Just listen to the children sing to you.

Fifth and Sixth Graders
    Jesus loves you, this we know
    For the Spirit told us so.
    Open and repentant hearts, he will never tear apart.
    Yes, Jesus loves you. Yes, Jesus loves you.
    Yes, Jesus loves you, the Spirit told us so.

Mr. Lost N. Foundit: It's not by chance that you came to this place to arrange this Holiday Tour today, Ms. Arranger.

Ms. Arranger: I'm beginning to understand. God's Spirit is at work in me, helping me to realize I can't keep Jesus just in the nativity scene. He's got to be allowed to enter every part of our lives — not just here in this church or manger scene, but out there in the world.

Mr. Lost N. Foundit: Yes. Jesus appears in every place through people like you and me who love others as we have been loved. Yes, Jesus loves us. The Light of God's love came into the world

15

in a tiny baby born in a manger, and the darkness that kept us from experiencing God's great gift is now dispelled. What better time to realize this than at Christmas. As we hear the story of his birth again, let us all remember to let Jesus' light shine upon our hearts.

Reader 1:   Luke 2:8-9
"That night in the fields near Bethlehem some shepherds were guarding their sheep. All at once an angel came down to them from the Lord, and the brightness of the Lord's glory flashed around them. The shepherds were frightened."

Reader 2:   Luke 2:10-12
"But the angel said, 'Don't be afraid! I have good news for you, which will make everyone happy. This very day in King David's hometown, a Savior was born for you. He is Christ the Lord. You will know who he is, because you will find him dressed in baby clothes and lying on a bed of hay.' "

Reader 3:   Luke 2:13-14
"Suddenly many other angels came down from heaven and joined in praising God. They said, 'Praise God in heaven! Peace on earth to everyone who pleases God.' "

Reader 4:   Luke 2:15-16
"After the angels had left and gone back to heaven, the shepherds said to each other, 'Let's go to Bethlehem and see what the Lord has told us about.' They hurried off and found Mary and Joseph, and they saw the baby lying on a bed of hay."

Reader 5:   Luke 2:17-20
"When the shepherds saw Jesus, they told his parents what the angel had said about him. Everyone listened and was surprised. But Mary kept thinking about all this and wondering what it meant. As the shepherds returned to their sheep, they were praising God and saying wonderful things about him. Everything they had seen and heard was just as the angel had said."

Ms. Arranger: Well, I thank you, congregation, children, and Mr. Lost N. Foundit, for helping me to realize that Jesus loves me, and I can't keep arranging my own life. I'll take Jesus with me from this day forth. He's set me free, so I guess it's my turn to free him to be God in this world and not just a baby in a nativity scene.

Mr. Lost N. Foundit: So let's go out as faithful children of God and adore Jesus, our Lord and newborn king.

(Exit Joseph and Mary, carrying baby Jesus, and Ms. Arranger, Mr. Lost N. Foundit, and Fifth and Sixth Graders as congregation sings.)

Closing Carol   "Oh, Come, All Ye Faithful"

Benediction

Offering

Bulletin

You Can't Keep Jesus In The Nativity Scene

Sunday School Christmas Program

Christmas Prelude   Youth Musicians

Welcome and Announcements
                                   Sunday School Superintendent

Opening Prayer   Pastor

Special Music

Opening Reader   Matthew 4:16-17

Ms. Arranger

Congregation   "O Little Town Of Bethlehem"
O little town of Bethlehem,
How still we see thee lie!
Above thy deep and dreamless sleep
The silent stars go by;
Yet in thy dark streets shineth
The everlasting light.
The hopes and fears of all the years
Are met in thee tonight.

O holy Child of Bethlehem,
Descend to us we pray;
Cast out our sins, and enter in,
Be born in us today.
We hear the Christmas angels
The great glad tidings tell;
Oh, come to us, abide with us,
Our Lord Emmanuel!

19

Ms. Arranger

Pre-school, Kindergarten, and First Grade
"Away In A Manger"

Ms. Arranger

Youth   "Jesus Loves Me"

Ms. Arranger

Congregation   "God Rest Ye Merry Gentlemen"
God rest ye merry gentlemen
Let nothing you dismay
For Jesus Christ our Savior
Was born on Christmas Day
To save us all from Satan's power
When we were gone astray.
Oh, tidings of comfort and joy,
Comfort and joy,
Oh, tidings of comfort and joy.

From God our heavenly Father
A blessed angel came,
And unto certain shepherds
Brought tidings of the same,
How that in Bethlehem was born
The Son of God by name.
Oh, tidings of comfort and joy,
Comfort and joy,
Oh, tidings of comfort and joy.

Ms. Arranger

Congregation   "What Child Is This?"
    What child is this, who, laid to rest,
    On Mary's lap is sleeping?
    Whom angels greet, with anthems sweet
    While shepherds watch are keeping?
    This, this is Christ the king,
    Whom shepherds guard and angels sing;
    Haste, haste, to bring him laud,
    The babe, the son of Mary!

    Why lies he in such mean estate
    Where ox and ass are feeding?
    Good Christian, fear; for sinners here
    The silent Word is pleading.
    Nails, spear shall pierce him through,
    The cross be borne for me, for you;
    Hail, hail the Word made flesh,
    The babe, the son of Mary.

Second Graders   "Hark! The Herald Angels Sing"

Ms. Arranger and Mr. Lost N. Foundit

Second Graders   "Jesus Loves Me"

Ms. Arranger

Congregation   "It Came Upon The Midnight Clear"
    It came upon the midnight clear,
    That glorious song of old,
    From angels bending near the earth
    To touch their harps of gold:
    "Peace on the earth, good will to men,
    From heaven's all gracious king."
    The world in solemn stillness lay
    To hear the angels sing.

For lo! The days are hast'ning on,
By prophets seen of old
When with the ever circling years
Shall come the time foretold;
When peace shall over all the earth
Its ancient splendors fling,
And all the world give back the song
Which now the angels sing.

Ms. Arranger and Mr. Lost N. Foundit

Congregation   "The First Noel"
The first Noel the angel did say
Was to certain poor shepherds in
Fields as they lay;
In fields where they lay
Keeping their sheep,
On a cold winter's night
That was so deep.

CHORUS: Noel, Noel, Noel, Noel!
Born is the King of Israel.

They look-ed up and saw a star
Shining in the east beyond them far;
And to the earth it gave great light,
And so it continued both
Day and night.

CHORUS

Third and Fourth Graders   "O Come, Little Children"

Ms. Arranger

Third and Fourth Graders   "Jesus Loves Me"

Ms. Arranger and Mr. Lost N. Foundit

Congregation   "The First Noel"
    And by the light of that same star
    Three Wise men came from country far;
    To seek for a king was their intent,
    And to follow the star wherever it went.

    CHORUS: Noel, Noel, Noel, Noel!
    Born is the King of Israel.

    This star drew near to the northwest,
    O'er Bethlehem it took its rest;
    And there it did both stop and stay
    Right over the place where Jesus lay.

    CHORUS

Mr. Lost N. Foundit and Ms. Arranger

Congregation   "Angels We Have Heard On High"
    Angels we have heard on high,
    Sweetly singing o'er the plains,
    And the mountains in reply
    Echoing their joyous strains.

    CHORUS: Gloria in excelsis Deo;
    Gloria in excelsis Deo.

    Shepherds, why this jubilee?
    Why your joyous strains prolong?
    What the gladsome tidings be
    Which inspire your heaven'ly song?

    CHORUS

Come to Bethlehem and see
Him whose birth the angels sing;
Come, adore on bended knee
Christ the Lord, the newborn king.

CHORUS

Fifth and Sixth Graders   "Good Christian Friends, Rejoice"

Ms. Arranger and Mr. Lost N. Foundit

Fifth and Sixth Graders   "Jesus Loves You"

Mr. Lost N. Foundit and Ms. Arranger

Reader 1   Luke 2:8-9

Reader 2   Luke 2:10-12

Reader 3   Luke 2:13-14

Reader 4   Luke 2:15-16

Reader 5   Luke 2:17-20

Ms. Arranger and Mr. Lost N. Foundit

Closing Carol   "Oh, Come, All Ye Faithful"
Oh, come, all ye faithful,
Joyful and triumphant!
Oh, come ye, Oh, come ye
To Bethlehem;
Come and behold him,
Born the king of angels.

CHORUS: Oh, come, let us adore him,
Oh, come, let us adore him,
Oh, come let us adore him,
Christ the Lord.

Sing, choirs of angels,
Sing in exultation;
Sing, all ye citizens
Of heav'n above!
Glory to God
Glory in the highest.

CHORUS

Yea, Lord, we greet thee,
Born this happy morning;
Jesus, to thee be glory giv'n!
Word of the Father,
Now in flesh appearing.

CHORUS

Benediction
Pastor: Go with the peace found in the Christ Child of Bethlehem, freed from all bondage. Go as the faithful proclaiming the Good News of Christmas. Go and serve the newborn King.

Congregation: Thanks be to God!

Everyone is invited downstairs for a time of fellowship and goodies.

Offering may be placed in the plates at the back of the church.

Leader's Helps

You Can't Keep Jesus In The Nativity Scene

Music

Special Music:
Special music may be played as a prelude before the program begins. Recruit youth musicians.
Special music may be inserted in the program to set appropriate mood.

Congregational Singing:
Opening Carol: "O Little Town Of Bethlehem"
"God Rest Ye Merry Gentlemen"
"What Child Is This?" (vv. 1 and 2)
"It Came Upon The Midnight Clear" (vv. 1 and 4)
"The First Noel" (vv. 1 and 2)
"The First Noel" (vv. 3 and 4)
"Angels We Have Heard On High" (vv. 1, 2, and 3)
Closing Carol: "Oh, Come, All Ye Faithful"

Youth Singing:
Words may be copied onto red construction paper for youth to hold if they need — class song and words to "Jesus Loves Me."

Pre-school, Kindergarten, and First Grade:
"Away In A Manger"
Away in a manger, no crib for his bed,
The little Lord Jesus laid down his sweet head;
The stars in the sky looked down where he lay,
The little Lord Jesus asleep on the hay.

The cattle are lowing; the poor baby wakes,
But little Lord Jesus no crying he makes.
I love you, Lord Jesus; look down from the sky
And stay by my cradle till morning is nigh.

Be near me, Lord Jesus; I ask you to stay
Close by me forever and love me, I pray.
Bless all the dear children in your tender care
And fit us for heaven to live with you there.

One verse of "Jesus Loves Me"
Jesus loves me, this I know,
For the Bible tells me so.
Little ones to him belong;
They are weak, but he is strong.
Yes, Jesus loves me,
Yes, Jesus loves me,
Yes, Jesus loves me,
The Bible tells me so.

Second Graders: "Hark! The Herald Angels Sing" (vv. 1 and 3)
Hark! The herald angels sing,
"Glory to the newborn king;
Peace on earth, and mercy mild,
God and sinners reconciled."
Joyful, all you nations, rise;
Join the triumph of the skies;
With angelic hosts proclaim,
"Christ is born in Bethlehem."

Refrain: Hark! The herald angels sing,
"Glory to the newborn king!"

Hail the heav'n born Prince of Peace!
Hail the sun of righteousness!
Light and life to all he brings,
Ris'n with healing in his wings.
Mild he lays his glory by,
Born that we no more may die,
Born to raise each child of earth,
Born to give us second birth.

Refrain: Hark! The herald angels sing,
"Glory to the newborn king!"

One verse of "Jesus Loves Me"

Third and Fourth Graders: Oh, Come, Little Children"
Oh, come, little children, Oh, come, one and all.
Oh, come to the cradle in Bethlehem's stall!
Come, look in the manger there sleeps on the hay,
An infant so lovely, in light bright as day.

Oh, see where he's lying, the heavenly boy!
Here Joseph and Mary behold him with joy:
The shepherds have come, and are kneeling in prayer,
While songs of the angels float over him there.

Oh, bow with the shepherds on low bended knee,
With hearts full of thanks for the gifts which you see!
Come, lift up your voices the child to adore!
Sing joy to the world, love and peace evermore.

One verse of "Jesus Loves Me"

Fifth and Sixth Graders:
                    "Good Christian Friends, Rejoice" (vv. 1-3)
Good Christian friends, rejoice
With heart and soul and voice;
Give ye heed to what we say:
Jesus Christ is born today;
Ox and ass before him bow,
And he is in the manger now.
Christ is born today!
Christ is born today!

Good Christian friends, rejoice
With heart and soul and voice;
Now ye hear of endless bliss:
Jesus Christ was born for this!
He has opened heaven's door,
And we are blest for evermore.
Christ was born for this!
Christ was born for this!

Good Christian friends rejoice
With heart and soul and voice;
Now ye need not fear the grave;
Jesus Christ was born to save!
Calls you one and calls you all
To gain his everlasting hall.
Christ was born to save!
Christ was born to save!

Pointing to Ms. Arranger, Sixth Graders sing this verse:
Jesus loves you, this we know,
For the Spirit told us so.
Open and repentant hearts,
He will never tear apart.
Yes, Jesus loves you.
Yes, Jesus loves you.
Yes, Jesus loves you.
The Spirit told us so.

Readers

Six readers are needed for this program. The Sunday school
superintendent, who is already up front, may do the opening
reading. Choose readers from the sixth grade class for the other
readings.

Opening Reader: Matthew 4:16 -17
"Although your people live in darkness, they will see a bright light.
Although they live in the shadow of death, a light will shine on
them....turn back to God! The kingdom of heaven will soon be
here."

Reader 1:   Luke 2:8-9
"That night in the fields near Bethlehem some shepherds were
guarding their sheep. All at once an angel came down to them
from the Lord, and the brightness of the Lord's glory flashed around
them. The shepherds were frightened."

Reader 2:   Luke 2:10-12
"But the angel said, 'Don't be afraid! I have good news for you,
which will make everyone happy. This very day in King David's
hometown, a Savior was born for you. He is Christ the Lord. You
will know who he is, because you will find him dressed in baby
clothes and lying on a bed of hay.' "

Reader 3:   Luke 2:13-14
"Suddenly many other angels came down from heaven and joined
in praising God. They said, 'Praise God in heaven! Peace on earth
to everyone who pleases God.' "

Reader 4:   Luke 2:15-16
"After the angels had left and gone back to heaven, the shepherds
said to each other, 'Let's go to Bethlehem and see what the Lord
has told us about.' They hurried off and found Mary and Joseph,
and they saw the baby lying on a bed of hay."

Reader 5:   Luke 2:17-20
"When the shepherds saw Jesus, they told his parents what the
angel had said about him. Everyone listened and was surprised.
But Mary kept thinking about all this and wondering what it meant.
As the shepherds returned to their sheep, they were praising God
and saying wonderful things about him. Everything they had seen
and heard was just as the angel had said."

Other Participants And Props

Pastor — lights candles and Advent wreath. May say something before program begins. Opens in prayer.

Sunday School Superintendent — welcomes and invites congregation to fellowship coffee hour after program. Acknowledges musicians and participants.

Living Nativity — Mary and Joseph in costume.

Ms. Arranger — wears a hat decorated in Christmas fashion and red or green vest with button that says, Holiday Tours; carries a flashlight.

Mr. Lost N. Foundit — wears a trench coat, hat, and carries a baby Jesus wrapped in blanket; calling card.

Props — Chairs for Mary and Joseph to sit in by manger. Manger with straw in it. Note to be handed to Ms. Arranger. Portable microphones for Ms. Arranger and Mr. Lost N. Foundit will help them to move around during performance.

Offering Plates — place at the back of the church.

Ushers — to pass out bulletins. Use older youth from congregation.